If your child struggles with a word, you can encourage "sounding it out," but keep in mind that not all words can be sounded out. Your child might pick up clues about a word from the picture, other words in the sentence, or any rhyming patterns. If your child struggles with a word for more than five seconds, it is usually best to simply say the word.

Most of all, remember to praise your child's efforts and keep the reading fun. After you have finished the book, ask a few questions and discuss what you have read together. Rereading this book multiple times may also be helpful for your child.

Try to keep the tips above in mind as you read together, but don't worry about doing everything right. Simply sharing the enjoyment of reading together will increase your child's reading skills and help to start your child off on a lifetime of reading enjoyment!

We Both Read: Amazing Eggs

With special thanks to Alicia Goode at the California Academy of Sciences
for her review and recommendations on the material in this book.

Text Copyright © 2011 by Fran Hodgkins
Illustrations pages: 3, 4, 7, 10, 14, 16, 22, 24, 26, 32, 35, 40, 41,
and Title Page Copyright © 2011 by Wendy Smith
All rights reserved
Use of photographs provided by Animals Animals:
Cover image: Zig Leszczynski; 2 © E.R. Degginger; 5 © Perry Slocum;
6 Michael Gadomski; 8 © E.R. Degginger; 9 S. Osolinski/OSF;
12 M. Watson/Ardea; 13 Alan B. Sheldon;
15 C.C. Lockwood; 17 O. Grunewald/OSF; 19 M. Chillmaid/OSF;
20 David Dennis; 21 OSF; 23 S. Dalton/OSF; 25 D. Fleetham/OSF;
27 R. Kuiter/OSF; 28 P. DeOlivera/OSF; 30 M. Fogden/OSF; 31 Patti Murray;
33 Maria Zorn; 34 Steven David Miller; 36–39 Highlights for Children/OSF
Use of photographs on pages 11 and 29 provided by Fotosearch.

We Both Read® is a trademark of Treasure Bay, Inc.

Published by
Treasure Bay, Inc.
P.O. Box 119
Novato, CA 94948 USA

Printed in Singapore

Library of Congress Catalog Card Number: 2010932586

Hardcover ISBN: 978-1-60115-251-0
Paperback ISBN: 978-1-60115-252-7

We Both Read® Books
Patent No. 5,957,693

Visit us online at:
www.WeBothRead.com

PR-11/10

Amazing Eggs

By Fran Hodgkins

With illustrations by Wendy Smith

TREASURE BAY

 Before you were born, you grew inside your mother. Your mother's body kept you safe and gave you **everything** you needed to **grow**. But most animals don't grow inside of their mothers. Instead, they hatch from eggs.

The egg has **everything** the baby needs to **grow**. The shell helps keep the baby safe.

Relative Size

Hummingbird egg

Ostrich egg

There are over 9,000 types, or species, of birds, and they all hatch from eggs. Bird eggs come in many shapes and sizes. A hummingbird egg is the size of a pea while an ostrich egg is the size of a large grapefruit.

Some bird eggs are blue.
Some have spots.

 Most birds build nests to hold their eggs. Nests can be made from sticks, grass, string, hair, or other materials the birds have **found**. Sometimes they are lined with soft feathers or plant fluff. Perhaps you have spotted a nest in your own backyard!

Nests can be **found** in trees. Some are **found** on the ground.

Bird eggs have hard shells. The hard shell and shape of the eggs make them strong enough for the **parent** bird to sit on them. Sitting on the eggs keeps them warm until the baby chicks are ready to hatch.

After they hatch, the chicks
are fed by their **parents**.

One bird that does not build a nest for its eggs is the emperor penguin. A female emperor penguin lays only one egg at a time. The male penguin keeps the egg warm until it **hatches** by holding the egg on its feet and tucking it under a thick flap of skin.

It takes nine weeks for the egg to **hatch**.

Birds aren't the only animals that lay eggs. **Most reptiles** do too.

Reptiles are a group of animals that have dry, scaly skin, breathe air, and are cold blooded. Reptiles include all types of snakes, lizards, turtles, and alligators.

Bird eggshells are hard. **Most reptile** eggshells are soft.

Alligator eggs

Alligators build nests and lay eggs in them just like birds. But alligators don't sit on their eggs. Instead, they cover them with dirt and debris to keep them warm. A mother alligator fiercely protects her eggs against anything that may try to harm them.

Alligators cry out when they hatch. The mother then digs up the nest to let them out.

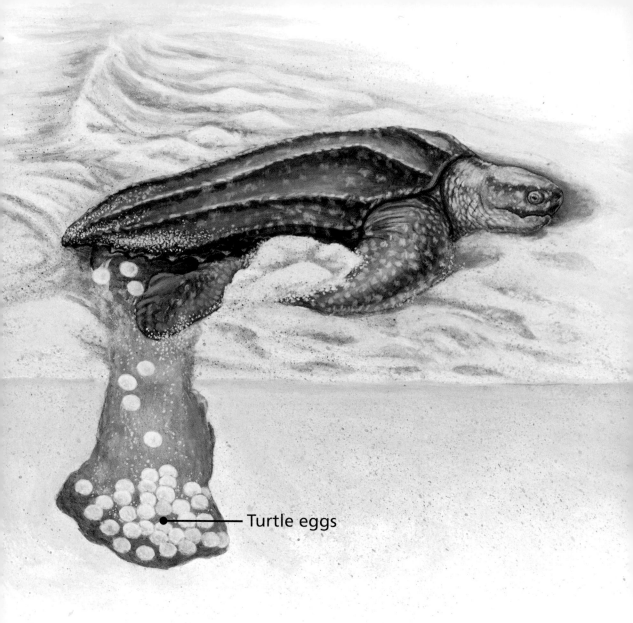

— Turtle eggs

Sea **turtles** come up onto the beach to dig deep holes, where they deposit their eggs. They bury the eggs in sand to keep them warm and hide them from other animals. Then the mother turtle returns to the sea, and the eggs are left to hatch on their own.

The baby **turtles** dig out of the nest. Then they run to the sea!

Egg tooth

The shell of a snake egg is soft and tough, making it difficult for the snake to break out. So, as a young snake develops inside the egg, it grows a sharp "egg **tooth**" on the tip of its snout.

The **tooth** rips the shell
to let the snake out.
Then the **tooth** falls off.

Amphibians, such as frogs, toads, and salamanders, are another group of animals that **lay** eggs. Amphibian eggs are different from bird and reptile eggs. They are small and have no shells to protect them. Amphibians lay their eggs in places that are damp, or in the **water**.

Most frogs **lay** eggs in **water**. The eggs look and feel like jelly.

Frogs don't look much like frogs when they first hatch. Instead, they look like little fish and are called *tadpoles.* Soon they grow hind legs and then front legs. Then their tails disappear.

Then they look like frogs. They can jump out of the water.

Fish eggs

Fish are another group of animals that lay their eggs in water. Some lay one egg at a time. Others can lay millions of eggs at once. Some fish eggs are very light, and they float through the water to hatch far away from **where** they were first **laid**.

Fish eggs

Other fish eggs sink.
They hatch close to
where they were **laid**.

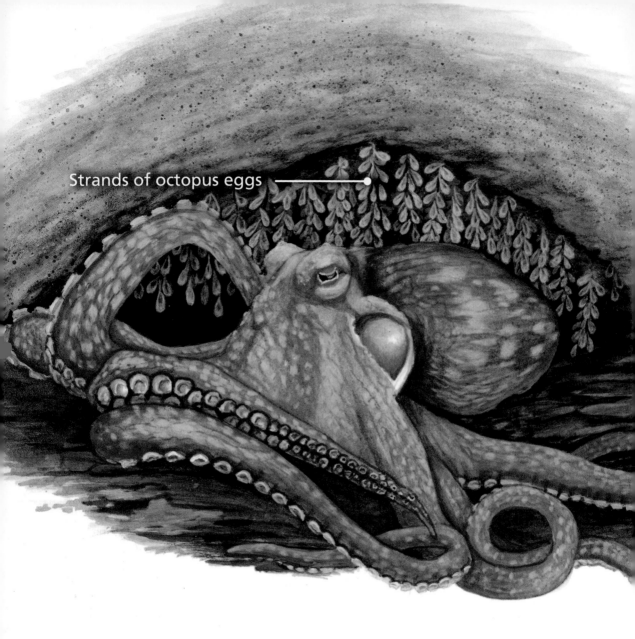

Strands of octopus eggs

Most of the animals in the ocean lay eggs. The **octopus** lays its eggs in a sheltering sea cave. The mother **octopus** stays with the eggs to protect them from other sea creatures.

These **octopus** babies are just hatching. Some **octopus** babies are as small as a fly.

   Certain **sharks** lay eggs that are unique.
They are rectangular and have long tendrils or
coils. These tendrils grab hold of seaweed or
rocks to keep the egg from traveling.

These eggs are often called *mermaid purses.*
Can you guess why?

Some **sharks** hatch from eggs. Some do not.

Extreme close-up of butterfly egg

Insects are the largest group of animals on Earth, and almost all of them lay eggs.

Have you ever seen an insect egg? Most are very tiny, but if you had a magnifying glass, you would see that some are very colorful and pretty.

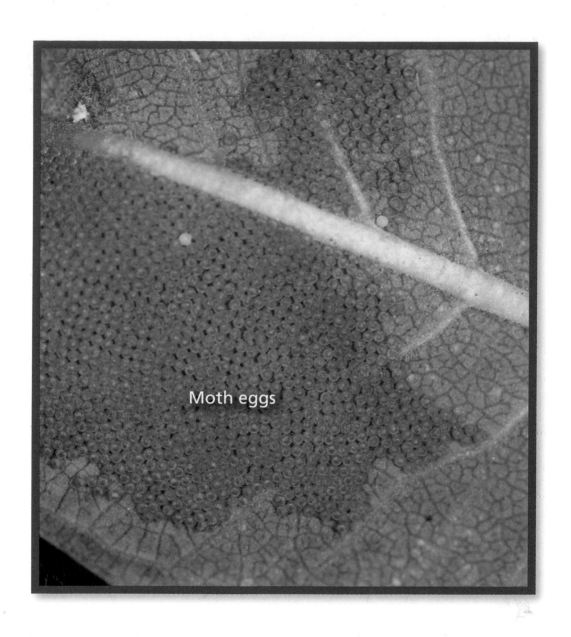

Moth eggs

Many **insects** lay eggs on plants. The eggs may just look like spots of dirt.

Bees lay their eggs in a hive. When a bee egg hatches, the bee first comes out as a worm-like *larva.* The larva matures into a *pupa* that looks like a white bee. Several days later it becomes a bee like the ones we see in our gardens.

Queen bee

One bee lays all of the eggs in a hive. She is the *queen bee*.

 Humans belong to a group of animals called *mammals.* Most mammals do not lay eggs, but there are a couple of exceptions. One of these is the **platypus**.

A platypus looks like a beaver with a duck's bill. Like beavers and ducks, it spends much of its time in the water.

The **platypus** lays its eggs on land.

Scientists believe that all **dinosaurs** hatched from eggs too. Even the huge, 80-foot-long brachiosaurus (brā′kē ə sôr əs) started its life as a hatchling!

Some **dinosaur** eggs were small and round. Some were big and oval.

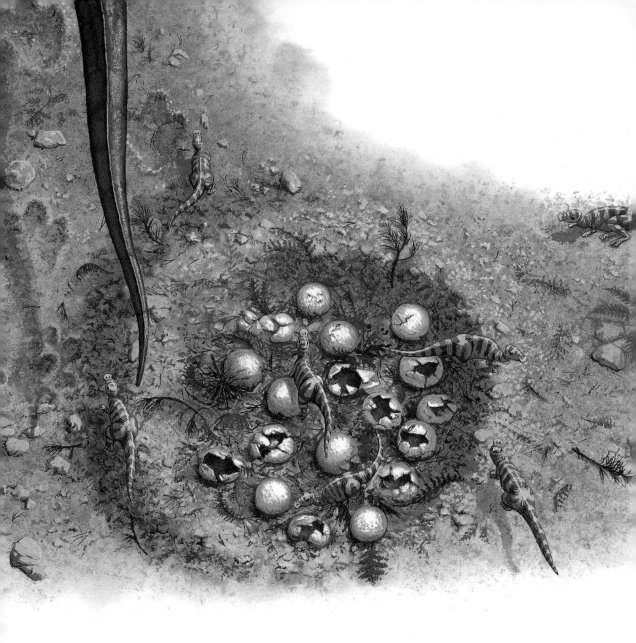

Fossils of dinosaur eggs and nests have been found in many places around the world. Scientists can learn a lot about dinosaurs by studying these eggs and nests. They now believe that some dinosaurs took good care of **their** babies after they were born.

Some dinosaurs left **their**
eggs to hatch alone.

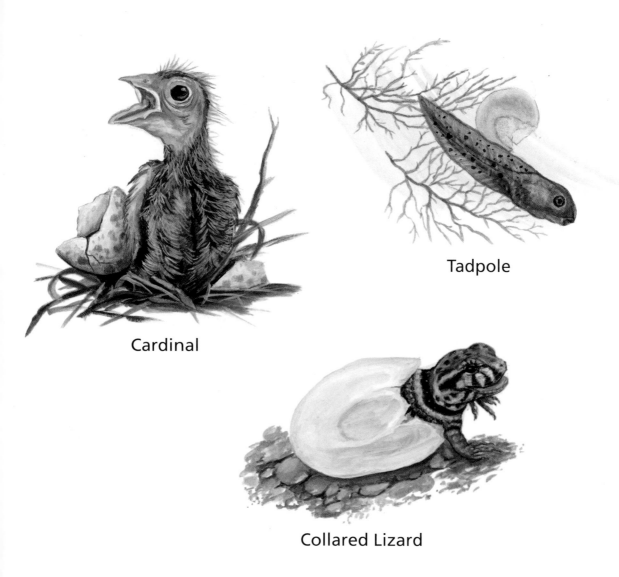

Cardinal

Tadpole

Collared Lizard

Eggs come in all shapes, sizes, and colors. They grow into tiny birds, giant turtles, colorful insects, and furry platypuses. Some are hard and some are soft. Some are big and some are so tiny that you can barely see them. But one thing is always the same.

Caterpillar

Hummingbird

Tortoise

Platypus

Eggs are amazing!

If you liked **Amazing Eggs,** here is another We Both Read® Book you are sure to enjoy!

Animals Under Our Feet

This book takes a close look at many animals that live or spend much of their life underground. It provides interesting information about why the animals go underground and how they live there. Animals covered in the book include the desert tortoise, moles, ants, meerkats, armadillos, burrowing owls, and many more.